IMAGES
of America

# SUSANVILLE

IMAGES
*of America*

# SUSANVILLE

Cheryl McCormack

ARCADIA
PUBLISHING

Published by Arcadia Publishing
Charleston SC, Chicago IL, Portsmouth NH, San Francisco CA


Library of Congress Catalog Card Number: 2007943614

For all general information contact Arcadia Publishing at:
Telephone 843-853-2070
Fax 843-853-0044
E-mail sales@arcadiapublishing.com
For customer service and orders:
Toll-Free 1-888-313-2665

Visit us on the Internet at www.arcadiapublishing.com

*To the Lassen Historical Museum volunteers, with their inspiring stories
of the past and idealism of preserving the future.*

# CONTENTS

# ACKNOWLEDGMENTS

I would like to extend my thanks to all of the people who donated pictures for this project and stories. Without them this book would not exist.

Many thanks to all who did not have pictures but who had wonderful stories of the past, including Evan Chappius, Jim and Jane Jesky, Lino Callegari, the Lassen Historical Museum volunteers, Marguerite Weir, Elizabeth Berti, and Carmela Surian from church, Becky Guess, the Lassen District Library, the California Highway Patrol, those I have not mentioned, and all those since deceased.

The Lassen County Historical Society and the Lassen Historical Museum have preserved many of the writings and records about Susanville and its residents' daily lives. Thank you for your tireless effort.

I would also like to thank my editor, Kelly Reed, for her understanding and help throughout the project. Lastly, I would like to thank my family and Michelle Brown at the Susanville School District for understanding my time constraints.

# INTRODUCTION

Hidden at first, untouched by the white man, the Honey Lake Valley provided food for indigenous tribes. With the discovery of gold, stories of hidden wealth in lands forgotten, and the promise of a new start, men came west looking in areas not yet traveled for a dream.

Peter Lassen, a self-made trail guide, was a rancher, miner, blacksmith, and sawmill operator. Well known for his travels into wilderness areas, William Nobles believed Lassen may have stumbled upon the fabled Gold Lake. Lassen took Nobles into the Honey Lake Valley and, instead of Gold Lake, Nobles found a shortcut to California. Isaac Roop, a resident of Shasta City, heard Nobles tell of his discovery. Looking for new possibilities, Roop traveled along Nobles Trail and made a land claim. In the future this land claim was to be the city of Susanville.

Roop built a house next to the trail, and it became a trading post for the wagon trains. He then dug a ditch to carry water to his house, and it was the first water system in Susanville. After much planning, a town grew around the trail from the fort up to the top of the hill. The trail became Main Street and Rooptown became Susanville. Roop constructed and operated a sawmill to provide building materials for businesses and housing. He also worked as recorder and postmaster until his death in 1869.

The area went through many legal squabbles about boundaries, which ended in the Sagebrush Rebellion. Roop's house became Roop's Fort after this, and Lassen County was named. Whether the name itself was what the settlers wanted they received the right to tax in their area.

Gold miners came to Susanville and moved into the nearby hills, creating small mining towns. The Chinese settlers set up laundries and restaurants near or in the mining districts. Susanville at one time sported two Chinatowns. Other immigrants came from Germany, Switzerland, and Northern Europe. People migrated from the eastern United States, and all had the common goal to build a better place to live and raise a family.

When women began to stay in town and raise families, a need was seen for churches and schools. Education was very important to the townspeople, and many of the political bond measures dealt with building or improving schools. Funds to build churches were raised but many people gathered together in whatever building was available. The town had saloons, hotels, stables, blacksmith shops, and general merchandise stores all along Main Street.

Outlying areas held ranches that supported the stores in Susanville. Transportation became a major industry because of the town's location. Location also encouraged food to be grown and raised locally. When mining towns grew in Nevada, the food surplus gave ranchers an economic boost.

Economic depressions led town leaders to look for new industries to keep Roop's dream of a town equal to San Francisco alive. In the 1900s, the railroad and two lumber mills brought people and jobs. However, fire was the catalyst that changed Susanville into a city. The city began to make improvements to its water and sanitation systems. Electricity and the telephone improved the quality of life, or so some say.

Then the automobile came, changing the businesses on Main Street, law enforcement, and recreation. Federal and state government offices moved into Susanville, employing more people. Life was full of promise after the Great War until Susanville encountered the Great Depression. However, people survived, and along came World War II. Job opportunities increased, and the lumber mills flourished.

After World War II, the mills slowly began to close. The city realized the need to incorporate the surrounding mill housing, and Susanville doubled in land size. Looking to keep the city from becoming a ghost town, city leaders brought in the state's prison system for employment in the form of a new correctional center.

Since its beginning, Susanville has looked for prosperity. The people come from many nationalities, work together, and belong to similar organizations. Disagreements and rivalries occur just like in a family, but the importance of American freedom runs the town.

# One

# EARLY SETTLEMENT

This is the inside of the Nathan and Schmidt General Merchandise Store on the corner of Main and Lassen Streets. Tillie Nathan is standing next to bolts of fabric and her son-in-law, Percy Chappius, is behind the counter. Tillie's husband, Marcus Nathan, came from Germany to Susanville to work with his uncle William Greehn. In 1877, Marcus started his own general store, which burned in the 1882 fire. He rebuilt and, in 1883, was open for business. Like many of the early settlers in Susanville, Tillie Schmidt Nathan has an interesting tale. Tillie's parents arrived by ship in New York; however, traffic was stopped because of a massive fugitive search. President Lincoln had been shot, and authorities were looking for John Wilkes Booth. After Booth was located, Tillie's parents continued on to San Francisco, where they opened a store. They stayed in San Francisco, and Marcus traveled there frequently to bring back merchandise for the store. Marcus Nathan died in 1913. His sons-in-law closed the Susanville store in November 1918 and moved it to San Francisco. M. A. Griffin moved his store into the building in January 1919. (Courtesy Rita Kahl.)

This is Isaac Roop's land claim registered in Shasta County. When gold was discovered at Sutter's Mill, more people flocked west. Peter Lassen, for whom Lassen County is named, made a long and hard trail from Oregon to his ranch at Benton City. The tale of Gold Lake prompted William Nobles to hire Lassen as a guide into the Honey Lake Valley. Nobles did not find Gold Lake, but he found an easier way for wagons and travelers to come to California. Nobles went back to Shasta and told everyone about his discovery. On June 14, 1853, a large fire burned Roop's business. Leaving Shasta City, Roop traveled along Nobles's route to the Honey Lake Valley and claimed land near the river. (Courtesy Lassen Historical Museum.)

Pictured here is Roop's Fort. Isaac Roop built a trading post for the wagon trains on his land. To encourage settlement, in 1856, Roop laid out part of his land into streets, which is now the uptown part of Main Street and Rooptown. Later the town was renamed Susanville. (Courtesy Lassen Historical Museum.)

Jim Byers operated a store and cattle ranch. In 1858, he began to buy land in the Honey Lake Valley and worked as a deputy for Plumas County. In 1863, the Roop's Fort became Fort Defiance in a skirmish between settlers and Plumas County. Byers worked for a compromise between the two parties. Lassen County was then formed in 1864. (Courtesy Lassen County Sheriff Office, Si Bollinger.)

MAIN STREET SUSANVILLE, LOOKING WEST

This view faces west on Main Street, where businesses came, stayed, and went. The Humboldt Exchange began in 1862 by John Burkett. In 1863, the saloon was sold and named the Pioneer Saloon. At the top of the hill is the Elks Building. Dr. Leonard first built the house in 1883. Other owners were William Greehn, Henry Swain, the Antlers Investment Corporation, and lastly, the Benevolent Protective Order of Elks in 1931. (Courtesy Susanville United Methodist Church.)

The first sawmill on the Susan River was built by Isaac Roop in 1857. Other sawmills were built later, including one mill operated by Ephraim and Luther Spencer in 1869. The Bremner Mill made apple boxes; apple orchards in the area sold produce in nearby mining towns in Nevada. (Courtesy Lassen Historical Museum.)

Robert Johnston was a farmer, hotel manager, and owner of the Johnston House. T. H. Long operated the hotel from 1901 to 1911, and then it was sold to H. C. Dobyns. Continuing to the left was a small restaurant, a fruit and vegetable market, and Frobel's Saddle and Harness Shop at the corner on the bottom floor of the Odd Fellows Building. (Courtesy Lassen Historical Museum.)

Kate Haley and Stephen Bass were married on December 25, 1883. The Bass family had a large ranch and farm between Johnstonville and Janesville. General mercantile stores and markets in Susanville bought fruit and vegetables from the Bass family and other area farms. In addition, Stephen Bass served as a county supervisor for 10 years. (Courtesy Lassen Historical Museum.)

Sol. Nathan's General Merchandise Store was at the corner on Main and Lassen Streets next to Johnston Hotel. A fire in 1895 burned the entire block. The Odd Fellows Lodge erected a brick building on the corner, and Sol. Nathan had his business on the first floor, sharing the space with other businesses. (Courtesy Susanville Historical Museum.)

The Smith Hotel was located on the south side of Main Street between Gay and Union Streets; it was a brewery in 1864. After the 1882 fire, the Oakes and Philbrook Furniture Store was built on the corner out of brick. In 1910–1911, the Bank of Lassen County moved into the building, and A. K. Philbrook built the first mortuary in the same block. (Courtesy Lassen Historical Museum.)

Standing in front of the old Emerson Hotel a group of men look at a German breed horse. The breed and quality of the horse were appreciated by many ranchers in the area. Roy Ramsey, standing third from the right, worked in the cattle business. (Courtesy Lassen Historical Museum.)

Inside the Pioneer Saloon Barber Shop in about 1903, Sam Dotson gives a haircut to George Armstrong. The other men, pictured from left to right, are Henry Williams, the owner of the Pioneer; Jake Cohn, general merchandise store owner; Dr. William E. Dozier, physician and surgeon; Fred Kingsbury; Frank Lane, bartender. (Courtesy Dr. John Dozier.)

The Hotel Lassen, formerly the Johnston Hotel, was renamed by the new owner, Henry Dobyns. On August 14, 1919, a fire beginning at Zimmerman's restaurant and saloon burned the block of businesses with the exception of Wood's Butcher Shop, a stone building. The inside of the hotel is pictured with the bartender, Louis Brashear. (Courtesy Lassen Historical Museum.)

Some of the early prominent men of Lassen County are pictured. Seated left to right are Robert Johnston, Loyal Woodstock, Frank S. Strong, William H. Jenison, Frank Thomas, Alexander T. Arnold, and Eber G. Bangham. Standing left to right are John Garrett, Wright P. Hall, John C. Davis, Abraham L. Tunison, Ephraim V. Spencer, William B. Long, Thomas Montgomery, and Dr. Robert F. Moody. (Courtesy Lassen Historical Museum.)

Susan Roop Arnold, the daughter of Isaac Roop, came to Susanville in 1862 and married Alexander T. Arnold in 1864. Susan was instrumental in the establishment of the Methodist church and Sunday school classes in Susanville. She was known for taking care of the sick and injured. (Courtesy Lassen Historical Museum.)

In 1875, the first Methodist church was built with help from E. V. and Luther Spencer. Bishop Bowman dedicated the church in 1877. Before this time, services were held in a variety of places. Itinerant preachers came from the Oregon conference and, in 1867, meetings were held in the newly built courthouse. (Courtesy Susanville United Methodist Church.)

Pictured here is the Methodist Gospel Male Choir in 1900. Around this time, the church and parsonage burned. Sadly, many of the church records were destroyed. The minister's family moved into a home on Cottage and Gay Streets. In 1902, a brick building was built for the church on the original site. (Courtesy Susanville United Methodist Church.)

Arnold's Planing Mill was at the bridge on the Susan River. L. D. Arnold came to Susanville in 1876 and, along with his father-in-law, E. P. Soule, he became interested in and took charge of the mill operations. The mill was a landmark in the county for 40 years before it burned in August 1914. (Courtesy Lassen Historical Museum.)

Pictured here is an early-day classroom in Susanville in the 1800s. A one-story schoolhouse, where E. P. Grubbs was a teacher, was built in 1863 on the southwest side of Cottage and Weatherlow Streets. In 1864, the county mapped the boundaries for the school districts. (Courtesy Lassen Historical Museum.)

Most Susanville Elementary School students walked to school. The one-story schoolhouse built in 1863 was removed, and a two-story schoolhouse was built in 1872. Both of these buildings were wooden and, in 1881, another classroom was attached to the outside. Nine grades were taught in the school. (Courtesy Lassen Historical Museum.)

Pictured here are students in the upper grades. In 1900, the schoolroom was heated by a wood stove. School usually began around 9 a.m. so children could finish chores at home and have enough time to walk to school. Students drank water from a dipper, a ladle-like spoon, out of a bucket placed in the main hall. Yes, everyone shared the same dipper and bucket. (Courtesy Lassen Historical Museum.)

In 1900, the second wooden schoolhouse was removed, and a two-story brick schoolhouse was built. Susanville Grammar School had six large and four small rooms. There were drinking fountains and no outhouses. Most unusual was the spiral fire escape in the back of the building. (Courtesy Lassen Historical Museum.)

In 1903, the grammar school expanded to include high school grades. These are the first high school students to attend the high school. Only two teachers taught all of the subjects, including Latin and German. Before high school classes were offered, many of the students went to San Francisco to complete high school, often boarding together in the city. (Courtesy Lassen Historical Museum.)

This is the first class to graduate from the high school. Pictured in the first row, from left to right, are John Long, Laura Long, Martha Hunsinger, and Winfred Riley. Standing in the back are, from left to right, Lola Hunsinger, Ralph Taylor, and Mabel Grass. The graduation ceremony was held at the Methodist church. (Courtesy Lassen Historical Museum.)

A new Lassen High School building was completed in 1906 with classes beginning on September 1, 1906. The building was constructed from native stone on the lower section of Main Street across from the skating pond, or "Frog Pond." The picture shows students walking to school. The extra-wide road is not yet paved, perfect for the cows strolling along with the lone car. (Courtesy Ron ReBell.)

In 1862, Thomas Newton Long (pictured) and Al Leroy built a hotel on the southwest corner of Main and Union Streets named the Magnolia. It began as a saloon, operated as a mercantile, and Judge Gordon N. Mott held court there in 1862. Long also operated a livery stable. Thomas Newton Long was sheriff from 1867 to 1871. (Courtesy Lassen County Sheriff Office, Si Bollinger.)

The Lassen County grand jury in the 1890s poses for a picture. William Williams built the first courthouse for $9,850 in 1867. To the right of the courthouse is the assessor's office. Behind the courthouse is the jail, from which Atlas Fredonyer, for whom Fredonyer Mountain was named, attempted escape while on trial in 1862. Fredonyer defended himself for four days while his cell mate was caught digging an escape tunnel. (Courtesy Lassen Historical Museum.)

Frank P. Cady, who served two terms as sheriff, from 1889 to 1892, is pictured in the sheriff's office with a Bank of Lassen County calendar above his desk. He also served two terms as county assessor before retiring from politics. With his son, Cady purchased and ran the electrical and water systems of Susanville in the early 1900s. (Courtesy Lassen County Sheriff Office, Si Bollinger.)

Oxen teams, such as this one going past the Methodist church, were used by the Anderson Mill on Paiute Creek. Ben Weisenberg is shown with the lead oxen, and Henry Vogt is on the load of lumber. Many of the other mills used horses and wagons to make deliveries. (Courtesy of Lassen Historical Museum.)

The U.S. Land Office operated from the Knoch Building. Standing in front of the office are T. A. Roseberry, Flora ?, and A. H. Taylor. Both Taylor and Roseberry came from Modoc County to Susanville. The U.S. Department of the Interior created the land office in 1812 to manage the territories and lands of the United States. (Courtesy Susanville United Methodist Church.)

Mr & Mrs T.A. Roseberry

Thomas and Viola Roseberry were married on May 22, 1877. Thomas was appointed to registrar of the U.S. Land Office in 1892, and they moved to Susanville. In July 1914, Thomas ran for county treasurer and tax collector but did not win the primary election. He died on August 22, 1915, while hiking Mount Lassen after its eruption. (Courtesy Roseberry House.)

Built in 1902 by Thomas and Viola Roseberry, this house stands on North Street at the end of Lassen Street. After her husband died and the Emerson Hotel burned to the ground, Viola remodeled her house and opened it for room and board. The place was first called the Green Tea House and later the Roseberry House. (Courtesy Roseberry House.)

Viola May Lowry Roseberry was born in Siskiyou County, California. At age 11, she moved to Modoc County and experienced the Modoc Indian War. Viola enjoyed painting oil landscapes, and many homes have enjoyed their beauty. She shared this love of painting by teaching classes first in Adin and then to high school and community college students in Susanville. She gave meals to many in need, including the local Native Americans, who gave her finely woven baskets to express appreciation. Viola compiled a book on her basket collection, which was shown at the 1915 World's Fair in San Francisco. She raised two boys and two girls. In 1915, she opened the Green Tea House in her home, which gave rooms and meals to boarders. Later the boardinghouse was called the Roseberry House. Viola died on March 24, 1936, and is buried in the Susanville cemetery. She is a true example of pioneer perseverance and charity. (Courtesy Roseberry House.)

In 1905, water pipes were brought into Susanville to upgrade the water system. Before pipes, residents put boxes in the water ditch to catch the water. The water ditch was first upgraded with wood and then terra-cotta pipes. The first ditch into town was dug by Roop from Paiute Creek to the fort. (Courtesy Lassen Historical Museum.)

This image shows merchandise brought into town by freight trains. General merchandise stores also delivered items to residents' houses. During heavy snow, deliveries were made by horse-drawn sleighs. At the time of horses and buggies, the dirt roads were dusty in summer and thick with mud in the winter. Some businesses built wooden sidewalks, which covered cellar openings and made for safe passage at night. (Courtesy Lassen Historical Museum.)

EMERSON HOTEL, SUSANVILLE, CAL.

The Emerson Building was built on the corner of Lassen and Main Streets in 1901. It housed several businesses, a hotel, saloon, dining room, and a store. There was one bathroom for every floor and a ballroom on the second floor. Charles Emerson also operated two ranches, three creameries, and a store in Standish. (Courtesy Susanville United Methodist Church.)

Charles Emerson taught school in Johnstonville and was principal at the Susanville Grammar School. His hardware store burned in the 1898 fire, and he built the Emerson Hotel in 1901. Emerson served as deputy coroner, two terms as assessor, and one term as sheriff. His official expenses for 1909 as sheriff were $1,510.82. (Courtesy Lassen County Sheriff Office, Si Bollinger.)

# Two

# LUMBER AND TRAINS

On April 26, 1913, the Southern Pacific Railroad completed the Fernley and Lassen Railroad to Susanville. In the beginning, a boxcar was used as the train depot with C. B. Morton as the first railway agent. The first train depot building was ready for use on September 14, 1913. Susanville Railroad Depot became a busy place, serving passengers and local shipping needs, and soon a larger facility was needed. In 1927, construction workers completed the new Susanville Railroad Depot. The old building was used as a storage shed while the new building included a baggage room, the agent's office, a waiting room, and bathrooms. The railroad was used for passengers and shipping freight. The rail line connected Susanville to Fernley, Nevada, and two passenger trains ran daily by the year 1918. Passenger service ended in 1933, as more people were using the automobile for transportation. (Courtesy Lassen Land and Trails Trust.)

After a big snow storm at the Susanville Railroad Depot, the trains still ran. The railroad brought a boom to the local lumber industry. Fruit Growers Supply Company and Lassen Lumber and Box each built tracks to connect to the main railroad. In 1979, Southern Pacific discontinued service to Susanville. (Courtesy Lassen Land and Trails Trust.)

Logs are waiting to be processed at the Fruit Growers mill. Logs were stacked by a steam crane on the railroad tracks, which took the logs off the railroad cars and placed them on the log deck. Beyond the log deck is the main office and the firehouse, which had two engines. (Courtesy George and Norma Stampfli.)

The Lassen Lumber and Box Company, established in 1918, built its mill at the end of Modoc Street near the new railroad. The train depot, powerhouse, and storing sheds are pictured here. The company had two mills, a box factory, and a planing mill. In 1950, Lassen Lumber and Box was sold to Fruit Growers. (Courtesy George and Norma Stampfli.)

Before the days of chain saws, the tree was first cut to make sure it toppled the correct direction and then it was cut with a saw. Some of the land where lumber was cut was U.S. Forest Service land. Lumbering helped prevent fires and keep the trees healthy. Too many trees caused drought and insect infestations. (Courtesy Lassen Historical Museum.)

This is the millpond at Lassen Lumber and Box Company. Most mills used water to clean the logs after they were cut. Since the area did not have the large rushing streams of the Midwest, millponds were used until technology changed. (Courtesy Lassen Historical Museum.)

This picture shows logs being moved by horses at Lassen Lumber and Box Company. Horses were used to skid the logs to the railroad. Lassen Lumber and Box logged up in the hills where horses also maneuvered better on the roads. All of the lumber companies had barns for storing hay and to keep their horses. (Courtesy Lassen Historical Museum.)

Logging camps like this one pictured in 1923 were used so loggers did not have to travel home far distances at the end of the workday. The trees were cut here and transported to the mill. Logging camps had temporary housing with a cook to provide meals. (Courtesy Julie McQueen.)

Railroad tracks were used to move the lumber to the mills. Rail lines were also built from the mills to the train depot to transport finished items easily. Improvements to roads in the mid-1920s allowed for lumber to be transported by trucks, and a new industry evolved. When the railroad closed, trucks took over the transportation of lumber. (Courtesy Lassen Historical Museum.)

Pictured here is a work crew for Lassen Lumber and Box Company. These men worked felling trees and moving them for transport to the mill. In the early days, this was manual labor because the men operated handsaws and axes. The Depression caused the mills to cut back on personnel. (Courtesy Lassen Historical Museum.)

This is the Lassen Lumber and Box office. At first the company rented the top floor of the Swain building, later called the Elk's. Ned Folsom from Susanville had been corresponding with Charles McGowan from Pittsburg on building a mill in the area. By 1918, McGowan notified Folsom that he would be arriving in Susanville. Lumbermen arrived from Pittsburgh, and logging began. (Courtesy Lassen Historical Museum.)

Pictured here is housing for the Lassen Lumber and Box Company. Charles McGowan chose a piece of land in the Lassen town site. The company constructed the millpond, railroad, and a small sawmill first. Then they began building a planing mill and box factory to supply wood for housing. (Courtesy Lassen Historical Museum.)

Ray and Anne Watts built their home at 608 Maple Street in the late 1930s. Ray was a manager at Lassen Lumber and Box Company, while Anne worked as a secretary for Hardin Barry, an attorney in town. Anne grew up in Madeline Plains. (Courtesy Julie McQueen.)

Pictured here is the Lassen Lumber and Box Conservatory. During the economic depression of the 1930s, the mill completely shut down. In 1936, the mill reopened under Horace Bridgeford and relied on the logging trucks to supply the needed lumber. Certain departments were leased to private entities. (Courtesy Lassen Historical Museum.)

An engine moves logs at Lassen Lumber and Box Company. The engines could maneuver on the railroad tracks and placed logs on flat cars that went to the mills. Some mills began to use gasoline tractors to move lumber from the loading area to the mill, replacing the horses. (Courtesy Lassen Historical Museum.)

A truck is taking a log to the Fruit Growers mill back when one tree filled up the back of the truck. Truck owners made contracts with the logging companies for hauling lumber to the mills. When the railroad crossing in Susanville became a hazard, restrictions were placed on the mills, which began to use more trucks for hauling lumber. (Courtesy George and Norma Stampfli.)

Pictured here is the Fruit Growers office staff in 1938. From left to right are Louise Saffores, Dan Moran, Gus Bishop, Art Lucero, Homor Vincent, Earl Buengham, Elton Millar, Jack Clark, Wally Harly, Glen ?, and E. D. Hunt. The company built dormitory buildings, a boardinghouse for the single men, apartment buildings, and company houses for the married men. (Courtesy Lassen Historical Museum.)

A sawmill crew is standing near the Fruit Growers mill. Behind them is the burner, which disposed of all the unusable material. After 1950, when pressboard became marketed, the mill began using all parts of the tree. Fruit Growers purchased the Red River mill in 1944 and Lassen Lumber and Box in 1952. In 1963, Fruit Growers sold their operation in Susanville. (Courtesy George and Norma Stampfli.)

Pictured here is the women's crew that worked at Lassen Lumber and Box during World War II. During the war, there was a need for packing crates, ammunition boxes, and military barracks. Like in other parts of the United States, women filled the shoes of the men. At Lassen Lumber and Box, the women sorted the box pieces to be assembled. (Courtesy Rufina Aguirre.)

A group of boys stands in front of the entrance to the Story Club. The Story Club was built by the Fruit Growers and housed a dining room, a game room, a library, and a large auditorium that was used for many events. There was also a barbershop and other stores. (Courtesy Lassen Historical Museum.)

The Lassen Grain and Milling Company was located on Richmond Road near the Susanville Railroad Depot. It had a flour mill from which grain grown in the Honey Lake Valley was ground. In the early days before the flour mill, there were gristmills. If there was no mill, people had to grind grain in a hand-held coffee mill. (Courtesy Lassen Historical Museum.)

# *Three*

# THE CITY GROWS

Fire was the biggest catalyst for growth. Pictured here is the Masonic building after the 1898 fire. An oil chandelier fell, scattering oil and starting the fire. The *Lassen Advocate*, the local newspaper; F. H. Bangham Store; the U.S. Land Office; W. D. Minckler, surveyor; J. E. Pardee, attorney; Goodwin and Goodwin, attorneys; and the C&O Telegraph Company were some of the occupants. David Knoch purchased the building after the fire and rebuilt it, and it was dubbed the Knoch Building. After 1910, a third story was added to the building. David Knoch came from Germany in 1853. The first few years he spent trading goods to the miners in the fields. Later with a horse, cart, and a safe, Knoch made a business "banking" the sheepherder's money and traveled to them—what service! Later Knoch owned the largest store in town. David's son, Isaac, and Jules Alexander opened Lassen Industrial Bank in the corner of the Knoch Building until a new bank was built. (Courtesy Susanville Historical Museum.)

This is the old Susan River Bridge. How precarious a situation to cross the bridge in a buggy! The bridge was wide enough for buggy-and-horse travel. It connected the gold mines of the Richmond Road district to Susanville. Repeated use caused locals to put up a log to help hold up the bridge. (Courtesy Susanville United Methodist Church.)

This picture shows boys cooling off in the Susan River while construction is taking place above on the bridge. With the new railroad and lumber industries knocking on Susanville's door, the bridge needed to be able to support heavier loads. The bridge was also widened to accommodate larger vehicles. (Courtesy Susanville United Methodist Church.)

Both pictures show construction taking place on the Susan River Bridge, which later became known as the Richmond Bridge. The bottom picture shows Washington School in the background up on the hill. Ralph Taylor, son of A. H. Taylor, constructed many of the brick buildings in Susanville and other towns. His dad worked at the U.S. Land Office and sometimes helped minister at the Methodist church. His uncle, Theodore Taylor, was pastor at the Methodist church. Ralph, who came to Susanville in the early 1900s, taught architecture at Lassen Union High School and Lassen Community College between the 1918 and 1953. (Courtesy Susanville United Methodist Church.)

At first called the Susanville Grammar School, the name was soon changed to Washington School. Washington School had a bell to call students to school and announce breaks for lunch. The bell was made by the Bell Founding and Brass Works in San Francisco and weighed around 70 pounds. (Courtesy Lassen Historical Museum.)

Pictured here are the fourth and fifth grades at Susanville Grammar School in 1919. With the opening of Lassen Lumber and Box Company, the enrollment grew rapidly. By 1920, discussion was taking place about whether and where to build another school. Local transportation was available for students living in the Milwood area of town on the other side of the high school. (Courtesy Lassen Historical Museum.)

In the early days, snowball fights were allowed at school. This is the boys' side of the playground at recess. When the weather was very cold, boys often played jacks indoors. Playground equipment was not provided by the schools so children brought their own from home. (Courtesy Lassen Historical Museum.)

The picture above shows the hospital first being constructed amid the cow pastures in 1915. It replaced the structure built in 1883. Pictured below is the completed hospital, whose superintendent was Ed Bass. Colds, coughs, and general ailments were seen in the doctor's office, though doctors also often traveled to patients' homes for medical visits. Surgery frequently took place in the nearest home. People used their own vehicles to transport patients. Dr. Fred Shanks is credited for bringing to town's first x-ray machine in the early 1900s. Blood pressure instruments came after 1915. Two of the worst diseases were typhoid fever and pneumonia until sanitation was improved. Before the sewerage system was installed, townspeople used outhouses, and some businesses ran sewage to the river. (Courtesy Susanville United Methodist Church.)

This picture was taken after the 1915 fire in Susanville. Fires were a major event in the West with the dry conditions and high winds. Isaac Roop's business in Shasta City burned in a fire. To prevent disastrous fires in Susanville, Roop made Main Street extra wide so the fire would be less likely to jump across the street. (Courtesy Susanville United Methodist Church.)

This shows the ruins of the Emerson Hotel after the 1915 fire, which burned the entire block of Lassen Street back to the Methodist church. The Hyer Hotel, the Methodist church, and Emerson's warehouse were destroyed. Sadly, the fire occurred on the birthday of Charles Emerson, the owner of the Emerson Hotel. (Courtesy Susanville United Methodist Church.)

The Methodist church is seen here being rebuilt after the 1915 fire. The first fire, which occurred in 1865, began in a livery stable on the corner of Main and Gay Streets. Businesses began to rebuild with stone or brick. However, not all buildings made of brick withstood the flames, especially with the roofing materials used. (Courtesy Susanville United Methodist Church.)

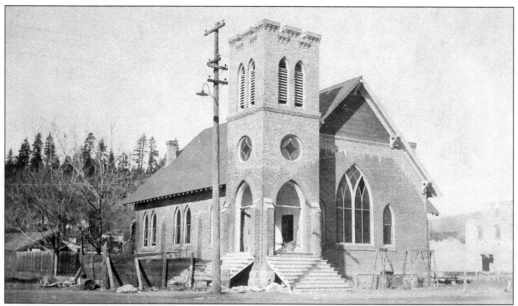

Above the newly reconstructed Methodist church is finished. When the old courthouse was demolished, the church retained its bell. At this time, several denominations had church buildings, including the Congregationalist church (built in 1878), Sacred Heart Catholic Church (first built in 1898), and the First Baptist Church (built in 1914). Many other churches were built in the following years. (Courtesy Susanville United Methodist.)

This is the Methodist parsonage. The first parsonage was built by Reverend Jennings in 1883. Then, in 1911, a new parsonage was built on Cottage Street next to the church. It was the first building in Susanville to be constructed by John Woodward. Later the parsonage was used as an extension of the church. (Courtesy Susanville United Methodist Church.)

Glayds Spencer Burroughs
1918–1919

Gladys Spencer Burroughs was the daughter of E. V. Spencer and the wife of Harry D. Burroughs. She graduated from Chico State Normal School in 1891, was principal of Susanville Grammar School in 1892, served on the school's board of trustees, was a member of the Susanville City Council, became the first woman mayor of Susanville in 1924, was a superior court judge of Lassen County, and was an assistant attorney general of California—a woman ahead of her times! Locally she was also a member of the Monticola Club and its involvement with the library. With a collection of books and a room shared with the chamber of commerce, the Monticola Club began the county's library. The first library rotated books among all of the schools in the area and continued to use the Monticola facilities. Miriam Colcord was the first librarian. In 1917, the library was moved to the basement of the courthouse with a branch on Main Street in the florist's shop. In 1920, the library moved next to city hall. Later the library moved into its own building behind the courthouse until the 1990s. (Courtesy Lassen Historical Museum.)

Julien E. Pardee moved to Plumas County and worked for Green Mountain Mining Company as a bookkeeper. He also worked for the Quincy Post Office before being named as the U.S. Land Office registrar in 1888. He began a law practice in Susanville and served in law until 1925. Pardee resigned as registrar in 1890 and was elected district attorney in 1892. In 1900, the city of Susanville became incorporated, and Pardee was named president of the city's trustees, an office later known as mayor. Pardee was also part of the Lassen Townsite subdivision, which ended up being sold to Fruit Growers. He was a member of the Masonic lodge, which Peter Lassen is credited for beginning in Northern California. After fire destroyed the wooden meeting place, the lodge erected a two-story stone structure, which became the Knoch building. (Courtesy Lassen Historical Museum.)

The picture above shows the old courthouse, built in 1867. In front of the courthouse, work has begun on the new structure. The first court, held in 1863, used the Magnolia Hotel and Saloon until the two-story wooden structure was built. In 1913, a piece of the ceiling fell and almost hit Judge Harry Burroughs, husband of Gladys, in the head. The bottom picture shows the new jail in 1916. Up the street from the jail is the cemetery, established in 1860 when Perry M. Craig drowned in a millpond. A fence was erected in 1864 and enlarged in 1879. Many of the people buried in the cemetery died from diseases due to poor sanitation. (Courtesy Susanville United Methodist Church.)

Pictured in front of the jail are Fred McClelland (left) and Bert Chappell, both of whom worked for the state's department of motor vehicles, which served motorcycles first, then cars. Fred was assigned his position in 1924, and Bert was hired in 1927 to patrol Westwood Road. The department managed the roadways until 1929, when the California Highway Patrol was created by state legislation. About 730 patrol officers enforced the road after 10 years. In small cities like Susanville, this extra uniformed presence helped the local sheriff and police. When the city of Susanville was incorporated, the first police chief was W. H. Edwards. During Prohibition, two of the police chiefs resigned when they were suspected to be participants in liquor establishments. (Courtesy Lassen County Sheriff Office, Si Bollinger.)

This is the finished courthouse in 1920. Before the courts arrived in 1864, mob hangings occurred. In 1863, Hon. John S. Ward presided. Other judges after him included I. J. Harvey (1864–1865), John S. Chapman (1869), Hendrick (1880–1885), Harry D. Burroughs (1909–1937), and Gladys Burroughs (1936–1937), who was appointed to finish her husband's term in office. (Courtesy Susanville United Methodist Church.)

Pictured here is the two-door county garage in 1920. With the use of automobiles increasing, the county decreased its use of horses and saw a need to house the vehicles used. Imagine using this in today's world of multiple-vehicle homes! (Courtesy Susanville United Methodist Church.)

Washington School, formerly known as the Susanville Grammar School, was red brick with a circular fire escape. To eliminate confusion, the new school building erected next to Washington School was first called the Susanville Grammar. Then the white-and-red schoolhouse was called McKinley School. Because of the population surge caused by new lumber mills, students attended classes in both buildings. By the end of World War II, Washington School was condemned for safety reasons, and McKinley School soon followed. The buildings were torn down, and one school originally called Washington School and later called Credence, was built in their place. (Courtesy Susanville United Methodist Church.)

This is Susanville's famous Bank of America building, which stood on the corner of Main and Gay Streets. The magnificent structure, complete with columns, belonged in a larger city. The bank became famous in town through its demolition, or attempted demolition, because the crew had a very difficult time knocking down the building. Across Main Street on the opposite corner stood the Bank of Lassen County, which merged with Bank of America in 1933. Across Gay Street from Bank of America was another bank at one time, Heart Federal Savings. Heart Federal was the site of Long's Livery Stable. Before the Bank of America was built on the corner, the corner contained farm items for the Alexander and Knoch Store. This was the site of Steward's Hotel, which was first erected in the 1860s but burned in the 1893 fire. (Courtesy Susanville United Methodist Church.)

Jules Alexander came to Susanville in 1877 and worked for the store Greehn and Asher. Later, with his father-in-law, he owned his own mercantile business called Alexander and Knoch. Alexander's son-in-laws operated the business after his death, and the store became Feher and Worley and was in business until 1942. Jules served on the Susanville City Council and was mayor in 1912. That same year, Jules and his brother-in-law, Isaac Knoch, opened the Lassen Industrial Bank, located in the Masonic building. The bank merged with Bank of America and was managed by Alexander until 1935. When Lassen Lumber and Box Company was looking to move operations to Susanville, Jules and Isaac Knoch owned the Lassen Townsite, upon which they built their business. Not as known are the improvements to the city Alexander helped organize, which include the paving of sidewalks on Main Street and the forming of the California-Oregon Telephone Company in Susanville. (Courtesy Lassen Historical Museum.)

Ingenious men thought hard and fast when rebuilding after fires. Building out of bricks or stone seemed to be a better way than wood, especially with the lack of a pressurized water system in the early days. In 1878, a brick kiln yard was built, but residents were not ready to commit to the expensive building material. (Courtesy Lassen Historical Society.)

This is the Manual Training Building in 1921. Lassen High School offered courses in building, architecture, and mechanics, as well as shop classes of various types. The classes often helped train students for jobs in local businesses and industries upon graduation. At one time, students worked with bricks like the ones shown in this picture. (Courtesy Susanville United Methodist Church.)

The Lassen High School class of 1923 is pictured here and shows how the population grew with the mills in town. Pictured, from left to right, are the following: (first row) Mildred Griffin, Homer Clark, Fern Bonner, Maylar Pullfora, Mary Brunhouse, Marie Doyle, Esther Wiencki, Auburn Jellison, Aileen Chittock, and Rensselear Brown; (second row) Burner Koken, William Dieter, Camille Elledge, Mabel Hamilton, Verna Winter, Odell Otis, Dorothy Tomlin, Eunice Cooper, Virginia Pettineli, and Kenneth Donaho; (third row) Bertha Hamilton, Irene Cramer, Hazel Doyle, France Gamma, William Price, Beth Hylen, Bryl Holmes, Esther Dieter, and Isabel Caughell; (fourth row) Fred Brockman, Clifford Bedell, Marion Silver, Lavern Jellison, Marge Wemple, William Scanlon, Melvil Dieter, Edna Hilderbran, John Cramer, and Florence Sorsoli. (Courtesy Lassen Historical Museum.)

The building pictured above is the agricultural building at Lassen High School. The other picture shows the agricultural class working in the fields. The fields were tilled and harvested by the agricultural class behind the high school building. The classes were a great opportunity for many of the students coming from the outer ranch areas. Students could experiment with growing techniques and new farming ideas without having to worry about not harvesting anything. Thanks to this and the classes offered in the Manual Training Building, students could graduate with education and training for a job without going to college. Later the fields and building were replaced with athletic facilities. (Above courtesy Susanville United Methodist Church; below courtesy Lassen Historical Museum.)

The top picture was taken behind Lassen High School and shows the facilities. The land was bought from Jules Alexander, and an impressive two-story building was built. Private property surrounded the east and west sides of the school. As the town grew so did the high school, which added new buildings. Education was very important to the townspeople, and the coursework equaled that of other towns and cities. As the high school thrived, sports became a source of entertainment and competition. The other picture shows students playing basketball behind the high school. The courts were dirt before they were paved. (Above courtesy Susanville United Methodist Church; below courtesy Lassen Historical Museum.)

The top picture shows the gymnasium also built by Ralph Taylor for Lassen High School. The gymnasium was located to the right of the high school when facing the school. It was later torn down to build the junior college. Pictured below is the 1923–1924 basketball team for Lassen High School. Thomas Long is one of the teammates. In 1940, the boys played football, basketball, track, tennis, and baseball. There were also boys' competitions in boxing, tumbling, and skiing. The girls competed among themselves in teams, playing basketball, hockey, and volleyball. Tennis, archery, ping pong, and badminton were also played. (Above courtesy Susanville United Methodist Church; below courtesy Lassen Historical Museum.)

This picture shows the water pump being tried out in front of the high school gym. This lower part of Main Street in front of Lassen High School was well known for flooding. In early days, people used to leave their homes and stay in the business district because of the impassable road. (Courtesy Lassen Historical Museum.)

Pictured here is Ralph Taylor's architectural model of the junior college. In 1925, the first college classes were held after high school hours on the Lassen High School campus. During World War II, enrollment increased due to the navy program. By 1966, the high school had been reconstructed, and it split from the college in 1969. By 1972, the college had moved to a new location. (Courtesy Susanville United Methodist Church.)

Lassen High School students are walking down Main Street past the St. Francis Hotel on the corner of South Union Street. William Koska began constructing the hotel out of concrete blocks in 1913 for the new owners, Flora and Bill Neuhaus. The new hotel opened its doors in 1914. (Courtesy Julie McQueen.)

Flora Neuhaus was the co-owner of the St. Francis Hotel, the second female mayor of Susanville, and the wife of Bill Neuhaus. As a child, Bill's leg was crushed in a threshing machine. Dr. William E. Dozier drove a team of horses 15 miles, amputated the leg, and Bill survived. Bill operated a pool hall for many years before he and his wife opened the St. Francis Hotel. (Courtesy Lassen Historical Museum.)

Ragnhild Hylen was born in 1900. Her father was homesteading north of Susanville in Madeline Plains and sent passage for the family to come to the United States on board the *Titanic*. Mrs. Hylen discovered she was pregnant and booked a different passage. Ragnhild, her mother, and her siblings arrived from England to join her father in 1912. Ragnhild was 12, and her mother believed in providing an education. At this time, the closest school was seven miles away in Ravendale. When Ragnhild and her sisters were ready to attend high school, they worked and boarded with a family in Susanville. Her mother decided to move to Susanville when the sixth child began high school. Her father joined them in Susanville in the 1930s when his health became worse. After high school, Ragnhild taught for a couple of years in Westwood and then studied at San Jose Normal School. With a teaching degree, she returned to Susanville to teach in the 1920s and taught until about 1952. (Courtesy Julie McQueen.)

Wright Spalding took this picture showing the snowfall. Ragnhild Hylen was boarding with Ruth Spalding at the time and received the picture. Ragnhild's sister, Beth, boarded with the Pardee family. At one time, Anne Hylen boarded with either the Knoch or Cady family, and Prudence boarded with Hubert Hill, who ran the Red and White Grocery. All of the sisters worked for room and board while attending high school classes. It was not until later that buses were used for transportation to the outlying areas in the county. All of the girls continued their education. Beth graduated from the University of Nevada, taught in rural Nevada, and then returned to Susanville to work for the phone company. Anne went to Healds Business College and became a legal secretary. Prudence finished nursing school at the Stanford School of Nursing in San Francisco, became a registered nurse, and then obtained a degree in public health nursing. (Courtesy Julie McQueen.)

J. A. "Gus" Pardee was born in 1881 in Plumas County and moved to Lassen County in 1888. He worked first for *Lassen Mail*, a local newspaper. Then Pardee went to work for Alexander and Knoch as a delivery boy. Pardee had some other short jobs before he went to study in San Francisco, and he took the bar exam there. After passing the bar exam, Gus returned to Susanville, married Blanche Spalding, and became a partner in his father's law firm. He served as district attorney and as mayor of Susanville. Pardee was instrumental in beginning the historical society in Lassen County by organizing several meetings, writing the bylaws, and finding meeting places. He also took time to write down the histories and convince others to write down their histories, thus preserving the past for the future generations. (Courtesy Lassen Historical Society.)

This is the Abe Jensen home built on Roop and Mill Streets by Ralph Taylor. Jorgen Jensen came to Susanville in 1864 and opened a blacksmith shop with William Brockman on the corner of Main and Lassen Streets. (This is the spot of the future Emerson Hotel and Mount Lassen Hotel.) Jensen and Brockman sold their blacksmith shop in 1866 and bought land located east of Susanville. A true pioneer, Jensen worked hauling supplies and then went into the cattle business. His son, Bert, sold part of his land to be used as the county's fairgrounds. In 1939, Delia Jensen sold her property to Abe Jensen. (Courtesy Susanville United Methodist Church.)

This is the home of Anne Swain in 1922. Anne moved into this house and rented out her original home at the end of Main Street after her husband, Henry, died. Anne rented the top floor to the management of the Lassen Lumber and Box Company in 1918 until office quarters were built at the mill. In 1922, the Antlers Investment Corporation purchased Anne's original home. Later, when the group became the Elks Lodge, the barn was torn down and an addition was built for meeting space. Many lodge members then desired to have the home torn down and replaced. A controversy arose with Med Arnold of the Lassen County Historical Society leading the fight to keep the historic building as a landmark in Susanville. (Courtesy Susanville United Methodist Church.)

Pictured here are William "Bill" Vellenoweth, known as "Dad Popcorn," and Lori Wright, who are standing in front of what was known as the "Little House on Wheels" at Gay and Main Streets. Bill worked as a ship's carpenter before coming to Susanville. He was well known for selling popcorn in front of the Spalding Drug Store. Bill also had a carpentry shop. This photograph was taken by George McDow. (Courtesy Lassen Historical Museum, donated by Mrs. Long.)

The Mountain Meadow Band is pictured here. Their leader is John B. Spalding. On the second row third from the left is J. B. Spalding and fourth from the left is J. A. "Gus" Pardee. On the third row first from the left is Ted Cady. The child has been identified by the donor as Mervin Spalding. (Courtesy Lassen Historical Museum.)

John Bridger Spalding was the son of Dr. Zetus Spalding, the founder of Spalding Drug Store. Spalding owned the store after his father's death. He also was an agent for Wells Fargo Express, a member of the chamber of commerce, and a mayor of Susanville. Zetus, his father, received his medical degree from Cleveland Medical College in Ohio. In 1865, Dr. Zetus Spalding came to Susanville and began a drugstore with his brother-in-law, A. C. Neale. Zetus filled the prescriptions and was the first doctor in town. In 1867, Zetus became sole owner, and his son, John Bridger, became his partner. Zetus, who also served as the county superintendent of schools, coroner, and public administrator, drowned in 1898. The drugstore burned twice when located on the north side of Main Street. In 1894, the business rented part of the Nathan Building until 1907, when their stone building next door was completed. During the summer of 1913, the drugstore got a new soda fountain, which employed many of the young people. (Courtesy Lassen Historical Museum.)

AFTER THE BIG STORM
SUSANVILLE, CALIF. 1922

This picture was taken after the big snowstorm in 1922. Before automobiles were used, horses pulled sleighs through the snow. Teenagers gathered together to take sleigh rides around the area and visit nearby homes. During deep snowfalls, paths were shoveled to move from one house to the next. Horses used the same paths, which were only wide enough to be one-way. Since there was little traffic on the roads, children sledded down the middle of the streets. Automobiles caused a problem because they did not travel well through snow. There were no studded tires, chains, or four-wheel drive vehicles. At first, owners of cars used horses and sleighs in the winter. When tractors became available, some streets were plowed. Eventually, as more people owned cars, plans were devised and people hired to plow the snow. (Courtesy Julie McQueen.)

Pictured here is the Charles McQueen family. In the first row, from left to right, are Charles, Marquerite, Francis, and Katherine. In the second row, from left to right, are Jim, Jack, and Baker. Charles McQueen came west at the age of 23 and ended up homesteading 160 acres of land in Bird Flat near Milford. Like many of the early homesteaders, the McQueen children impacted the town of Susanville with their employment. Baker McQueen worked in contracting and building, was the construction foreman at Paul Bunyan Lumber Company (a branch of Red River Lumber Company in Westwood), and mayor of Susanville. Marguerite worked as the bookkeeper at Sears in Susanville for 12 years. Jim worked as the agent for State Farm Insurance in Susanville, was president of the Susanville Rotary Club, chairman of the Lassen County Board of Supervisors, served on the Lassen County Fair Board, and was a member of the sheriff's posse. (Courtesy Julie McQueen.)

This picture shows the building of the Lake Greeno dam outside the town. An engineer named Schniedler and William Earl planned an earth-filled dam along Long Valley Creek in 1890. The dam was to send water through canals to both sides of Honey Lake. The local farmers formed a cooperative to construct the dam, and the McQueen family worked on the project. In 1892, the dam washed out. In 1915, the plan was to tap into the Little Truckee River drainage and channel the floodwater into the Lake Greeno dam site. This water was later diverted to Nevada. Bringing water to the outlying farmlands and to Susanville residents was a recurring issue from the time of settlement. Other water-bearing projects include the Bly (Eagle Lake), Amedee, Balls Canyon, and Skedaddle Creek. Many of the projects failed, and investments were lost. (Courtesy Doug and Lorena Millar.)

Pictured here is Jim Leavitt, a Lassen County sheriff from 1927 to 1934. Jim was sheriff during part of the Prohibition period. One local Prohibition story tells of Frenchie the Barber, an establishment frequently raided by the U.S. federal marshals. Frenchie had a pipe running to the river from his business. Whenever word came that the federal agents were in town, Frenchie poured the "stuff" into the river. He was never caught and became a great puzzlement to the officials. Leavitt also worked as a farmer and stock raiser. Jim's father, Benjamin, created one of the successful water irrigation systems in the county, which took water from the Susan River drainage basin down to Lake Leavitt out of Susanville. The engineer was James Elledge, who worked on many of the area's water projects. The company was sold in 1904 and renamed the Lassen Irrigation Company. (Courtesy Lassen County Sheriff Office, Si Bollinger.)

Pictured here is Sallie Norman, an elderly lady known as "Old Lucy" who was of Native American descent and who lived a nomadic lifestyle amongst the townspeople of Susanville. No one knew her exact age, but she was more than 100 years old when she died. Many Native American women worked washing clothes for households in the early days. Of course there are some famous Susanville Native Americans like Tommy Tucker, the first man from Susanville killed during World War I. In 1923, thirty acres of land were purchased from Mrs. Taylor as a residence for the landless and homeless Native Americans living in the area. Since federal money was used to purchase the land, the Rancheria itself had consideration as a tribe. This tribe was unlike other tribes under the Department of the Interior because many different groups lived and participated in the Rancheria's membership. Through a long political process, the Rancheria's charter was recognized in 1969 by the U.S. Department of the Interior. (Courtesy Lassen Historical Museum.)

# *Four*

# CHANGES

Pictured here is the Lassen Electric Company in 1931. Standing from left to right are Ted Cady, owner; Sam Thomas; Agatha Kramer, counter; Mervin McKenzie, books; Percy Haling; Frank Burnett, water department. In the 1890s, James Anthony supplied hydroelectric power from the Susan River to town businesses. In 1897, Anthony sold his business to A. J. Nourse, who added improvements and operated the business until 1900. James Branham bought the plant and operated it until his death, upon which Isaac Knoch acquired the facility. Knoch sold the business to the Lassen Electric Company in 1913. The electric company was becoming overloaded with the population growth of the mills and was sold to the Red River Lumber Company with Cady continuing as manager. The lumber company's surplus power supplemented the power to Susanville so well that power lines were put up into the Honey Lake Valley. (Courtesy Lassen Historical Museum.)

This is a picture of the 20/30 Club in Susanville in the early 1930s. Pictured from left to right are Charly Gorman, Murray Doyle, Howard Thornbill, Lawrence Hill, Lawrence Hemler, Al Bantley, Eddie Long, George Sorsoli, Carl Davis, John Greig, Bob Bankhead, James Bronson, Charles Gasko, Ralph Allen, Mervin McKenzie, Ivor Lanigar, Walter Agee, Nolan Hallowell, and Llewllyn Mathews. Mervin McKenzie was the bookkeeper at Lassen Electric Company. Ivor Lanigar began working at the post office in 1925. In 1942, Ivor was appointed first assistant postmaster for the Susanville office. In 1947, he became acting postmaster and was appointed as postmaster in 1948 by President Truman. Lanigar served as a volunteer firefighter for 13 years, was a member of the Elks Lodge, and was involved in the World War II bond drive. (Courtesy Lassen Historical Museum.)

This is a picture of the Fruit Growers Band in 1933. Many groups of musicians met together and formed bands. Often there were plenty of musicians but not enough conductors or teachers. Large bands were seen playing and marching in the parades. Small bands played for the many dances and events held. (Courtesy Lassen Historical Museum.)

This picture shows a class at Lassen High School in 1939. Subjects offered included English, languages, history, mathematics, sciences, agriculture, home economics, shop, mechanical drawing, physical education, art, and music. Students did not need to board with families in town anymore because the high school had buses and employed bus drivers. (Courtesy Julie McQueen.)

The picture above shows one of the many classes Ragnhild Hylen taught in Susanville. The picture below shows Lincoln School in the 1940s. With the population growth from the mills, the Lincoln School was built on Main Street by Woodward and Greebe in the Milwood Tract. L. D. McDow was the original pioneer owner and built his house in 1877 on the lot of the new Lincoln School site. In the 1920s, the Susanville School District decided to make more community schools that were in close walking distance for the neighborhood children. Lincoln School opened in 1923. (Above courtesy Julie McQueen; below courtesy Lassen Historical Museum.)

The public swimming hole is pictured here. Well into the early 1900s, children were allowed to swim in the Susan River. With more people visiting the river, a special place was designated for swimming and was donated for a public swimming hole. The Monticola Club organized the community to improve the small area. The picture shows a wooden ledge swimmers could jump off of into the river water. Before the public swimming hole, children often visited the river during the hot days. Many children played in areas of swift running water or jumped off high ledges into shallow areas below. Mothers often warned children not to go down to the river or creek to play and were often ignored. The river could be a fun place to play, but it could also be deadly. Diseases like typhoid were very contagious in the summer. (Courtesy Lassen Historical Museum.)

Both pictures show Roosevelt Pool before it was enclosed and became an indoor swimming pool. The pool would not have materialized without President Roosevelt's New Deal program. Many community members proposed ideas about places to build a pool and what the pool should look like without careful planning. In 1936, the city presented a plan for a municipal swimming pool to the Works Projects Administration, a New Deal program. The pool would use the natural hot springs for heated water. Plans were finalized, and the pool was built behind Roosevelt School on Richmond Road. The completed pool opened in 1938. (Courtesy Susanville United Methodist Church.)

This picture shows people ice skating on Eagle Lake. After automobiles made travel faster, people could enjoy recreational activities in the surrounding areas. Before traveling to Eagle Lake, ice skaters enjoyed the skating pond and the nearby millponds in Susanville. The skating pond was located across from the high school until the property was sold. Ice on the millponds and local lakes was cut for the local icehouses. Later ice was placed in household iceboxes, the precursor to the refrigerator. With the advent of electricity, the refrigerator displaced the need for ice cutters, and more frozen water was available for recreational purposes. Other winter activities included sledding and skiing. Children would sled down Main Street in the winter in the days before automobiles. They only needed to be wary of the evening stage coach. Some people would go skiing at Coppervale, north of Susanville. Others would use skis as a means of travel. (Courtesy Julie McQueen.)

The picture above shows a Lassen High School play. At this time, the senior and junior classes each put on a play for the public to attend. These plays were looked forward to by the townspeople. The high school also presented a Christmas pageant. The high school band in 1940 had 60 instruments played. The high school chorus in 1940 performed with the band in the Christmas pageant and Easter services. Pictured at left is James Ducasse, the son of Art and Beth Ducasse. James is also pictured in the class play above. After graduating from high school, James practiced dentistry in Watsonville. (Courtesy Julie McQueen.)

Who said school was all work and no play in the early days? Both pictures show students dressed for a class play in elementary school. What creative costumes the students are wearing! Most neighborhood grammar schools had graduation exercises during which students showcased their knowledge. In many of the smaller schools, students put on a play where everyone had a part. In larger schools, grades or classes scheduled events to show expertise in memorization, composition, and showmanship. Everyone looked forward to the performances. Later graduation exercises only encompassed the last grade attended at the school. (Courtesy Julie McQueen.)

Eleanora Dieter grew up in Standish and Janesville and began high school in 1920. Students went to school by car, often taking other students with them, for which a rider had to pay the driver. Eleanora married Cyril Houghton in 1923. After marrying, Cyril and Eleanora traveled to Southern California, where Cyril worked in construction. In 1924, they moved to Westwood, where Cyril worked for Red River Lumber Company. About 1926, the Houghtons moved back to the Honey Lake Valley and worked ranching. The Houghtons bought a house on River Street, now Gilman Street, in Susanville and, when the Great Depression came, Cyril was again out of work. The family started with two cows and went into the dairy business in 1932. This business was called Cy's Dairy. They rented the frog pond meadow, later Memorial Park, for pasture in the summer and the apple orchard on the river bottom all year long. (Courtesy Carrie Golden.)

In 1933, the Houghtons bought the meadow pasture across from the high school, and the dairy was renamed Cy's Dairy. The herd was increased to 18 cows, which gave very rich milk with one third of it cream. Milk was sold for 8¢ a quart and delivered to customers. (Courtesy Carrie Golden.)

A cow from Cy's Dairy grazes in the pasture. Behind the cow is the Veterans Memorial Building. In 1938, water breached the upper part of Paiute Creek and flooded the dairy. Cyril drove the truck to higher ground and moved the calves. Eleanora grabbed bedding and the baby. Fortunately, their dog, Shep, herded the cows all to safety. (Courtesy Carrie Golden.)

The post office was established in Susanville in 1859 and re-established in 1860 with Isaac Roop serving as postmaster. Mail was first brought to Susanville sporadically, especially in the winter. Then mail was brought by stage and the railroad. When the Nevada-California-Oregon Railroad came through Litchfield, Carl Arnold ran a stage to the station in the morning, picked up the mail, and ran the stage back to Susanville for delivery. The mail used post office boxes at this time. Before the post office building was built in 1938, when this picture was taken by contractor George Goedhart, the post office used a variety of buildings for its headquarters, including the Spalding Building and Knoch Building on Main Street. In 1925, carrier service was established in Susanville with men hired to deliver mail to houses. (Courtesy Susanville Post Office.)

In the beginning, postmasters were appointed every time a new president of the United States was elected. After Isaac Roop, William T. Ward was appointed postmaster in 1869. Trowbridge H. Ward became postmaster after his grandfather, William. John C. Partridge became postmaster in 1875, after serving as a U.S. surveyor. Albert A. Smith worked as county clerk and district attorney before becoming appointed postmaster in 1881. William D. Minckler was appointed postmaster in 1883 and served a short time before James Branham became postmaster in 1885. Charles Forkner was appointed postmaster in 1889. The postmasters appointed before 1933 were Nobel S. McKinsey, David C. Hyer, Frank Bangham, David C. Hyers, Ivor B. Clark, Chester D. Mathews, and Elmer R. Winchell. In 1938, when this May photograph was taken, air mail service began to deliver mail. What a difference from the early days! (Courtesy Susanville Post Office.)

Pictured above is Ruth Potter in her early years. Potter practiced midwifery around the mining camps of Utah. In the 1920s, her husband had a grocery store in Susanville, but during the Depression, he sold the business and went to work for President Roosevelt's work program. Potter decided to rent a building from Hal Story for a maternity home, to deliver babies. Of course, the resident doctors in town were skeptical at first and decided to test Potter. One day, a doctor came to the maternity home with a very pregnant lady and asked if Potter could keep her awhile because he had an emergency. When the doctor came back, the baby was successfully delivered. Potter later moved to a new location with five beds. The picture below shows Potter's Maternity Home at 1603 Main Street. (Courtesy Ricki Diamond.)

Pictured here are Art and Beth Ducasse, the owners of the State Café. The State Café was located on the corner of South Gay Street and Main Street next to the Grand Café. Before becoming a businessman in Susanville, Art raised quarter horses and was a skilled horseman. The Ducasses served food and liquor since it was after Prohibition. Beth worked for the telephone company. Telephone lines that connected Susanville to Quincy came in 1911. The first system connected all of the homes in Susanville to the valley. When the phone rang, everyone picked up the receiver until the party intended was identified. Residents never knew who was listening. In 1929, two switchboard operators in Susanville served 700 telephones. In 1951, dial telephone service began with six switchboard operators and long distance service. In 1964, some customers were able to direct dial while others employed the now 10 switchboard operators. (Courtesy Julie McQueen.)

The top picture shows the State Café Building. Beth Ducasse was a lady raised in the era of proper etiquette. One evening, a group of new teachers were having dinner in the establishment. When dinner was finished, one of the teachers came up to the bar and bought some alcohol. Beth, being the proper businesswoman, never said a word until she came home. She could not believe a teacher would drink in public. This was just not heard of, especially when she was growing up. How the world has changed! (Courtesy Julie McQueen.)

Pictured at right are Prudence (left), Julie
(baby), and Donald McClure. Prudence
Hylen McClure was the daughter of George
and Ann Hylen. She worked as a nurse at
Riverside Hospital and Lassen High School
and then became the head of Lassen County
Education Public Health. Donald McClure
came from Pittsburgh, where his father ran a
lumberyard. He worked as the bookkeeper at
Lassen Lumber and Box Company and then
the Union Station on the corner of South
Weatherlow and Main Streets. Ann Hylen
is pictured below with her granddaughter,
Julie, in 1949. Ann Hylen and her daughters
were instrumental in the establishment of
the Good Shepherd Episcopal Church in
Susanville. (Courtesy Julie McQueen.)

Pictured at left is George Woodstock and pictured below is his daughter, Gladys D. Woodstock. George was the son of Loyal Woodstock, one of the early pioneers in the county. Loyal served on the first board of supervisors for the newly formed county, the first grand jury, and as road overseer. He was a part of the Honey Lake Rangers militia in 1865. George was the first rancher to bring alfalfa to the area, farm the alfalfa for seed, and market it. The family is an example of many of the families that lived outside of Susanville but were involved by politics or business. (Courtesy George and Norma Stampfli.)

Pictured behind the counter is Leslie Mastolier, owner of Leslie's Jewelry Store. Mr. Murin, who operated a laundry in the back, is to the left. Leslie first came to Susanville in 1925 to work in the watch, clock, and jewelry departments of H. P. Jensen's store. Then Mastolier opened a store in 1930, specializing as a watchmaker and engraver. The store was briefly sold to W. H. Thornhill in 1946 while Mastolier supplied other jewelry dealers in Alturas, Portola, Quincy, Greenville, Chester, and Westwood from his shop at home. In 1947, Mastolier took over his former store. He served as a flight instructor during World War II for six navy aviator programs in Susanville, three army programs in Baker, Oregon, and 10 army cadet programs at Tulare. The store operated the longest at 612 Main Street when Mastolier was alive. (Courtesy Leslie's Jewelry.)

This picture shows the inside of the St. Francis Hotel in 1948 after it was remodeled by the new owner, Jane Goni. She is pictured with Steve Arainty and another chef. Jane Goni bought the St. Francis from Neuhaus on November 20, 1947. She came with her sister to Gardnerville around 1929. Upon her arrival, Jane worked off her passage to the person who bought her ticket to the United States. Jane married Eugenio Goni, moved to Smith Valley, and ran the Heyday Inn. She then moved her family to Reno and leased the St. Francis Hotel on Virginia Street. The Goni family owned the business for 53 years. Across Main Street was the Sierra Theater, which previously was the site of George Winchester's blacksmith shop. Up Main Street and next to the blacksmith shop was Long's Livery Stable. (Courtesy Lassen Historical Museum.)

Helen Sargent, owner of the Grand Café, pours refreshments for a customer. The Grand Café was first opened in the back of the Pioneer Saloon in 1909 by Kwan Wong and served American cuisine. In 1912, Wong moved next door in the new building erected on the site of the Pioneer Saloon's beer garden. In 1921, Steve Sargent and Sam Vucanovich took over the business. Steve married Helen in 1928, and she became a familiar face in the restaurant for more than 50 years. In 1934, the demolition of the Elite Café next door caused part of the building to collapse. Steve moved the Grand Café to temporary quarters, bought the Elite Cafe's property from Marie Doyle, and used both lots when he rebuilt his café. Like Wong, large numbers of Chinese came with the miners. The Chinese ran many of the laundries in town and worked in the restaurant business. The corner of Nevada and Union Streets was one of these Chinatowns. In 1909, Sacred Heart Church bought the lot and moved from their previous location on Richmond Road. (Courtesy Lassen Historical Museum.)

This is a picture of Purity Grocery Store on the corner of North Gay and Main Streets. To the left is part of the Bank of America building across North Gay Street. Upstairs from the grocery store were rooms, a lobby, and an office, so the building was often called the Home Hotel. Purity moved to the corner of Shasta and Cottage Streets, and later became another chain store, Food Lane. Another area grocery store was the Red and White, popular with many families because they took credit and delivered. The chain stores had the economic advantage during the Depression of pooling money from many locations to stay afloat. The first chain stores in Susanville operated within the local neighborhoods. It was not until the advent of the automobile that stores relocated within driving distance from neighborhood homes. (Courtesy Lassen Historical Museum.)

This is a picture from the Rodeo Parade in 1941. Louis Preciado is on the horse, showing off his horsemanship skills. Louis was a car salesman for Barron Chevrolet, previously called the Smith Auto Company, located on the corner of Main and Weatherlow Streets. The Smith Auto Company was owned by Ernest Smith, originally from Adin. The company sold cars for Chevrolet. Other car dealerships were seen in town. The Pontiac dealership was on the other side of Main Street from the Smith Auto Company. The Ford dealership, operated by Clemmy Doyle, Leland Hunsinger, and Cass Hunsinger, went farther up Main Street and took the place of Skaden's Livery Stable. Gradually all of the livery stables, blacksmith shops, and saddle repair shops disappeared from Susanville, having moved to the surrounding rural areas. (Courtesy Lassen Historical Museum.)

Pictured left is Art Ducasse (right) in one of the many Susanville parades. Art, the owner of the State Café, was an accomplished horseman before going into to the restaurant business. He managed sheep camps in the Madeline Plains area before marrying his wife, Beth Hylen. Pictured below are the fairgrounds for the Lassen County Fair in 1947. Before these grounds were purchased in the 1920s, the fairs were held in the Hall Street area. The Halltown fairgrounds had a racetrack and exhibit hall. Racing horses was a big event, especially up north in Bieber. (Left courtesy Julie McQueen; below courtesy Susanville United Methodist Church.)

Pictured here is the first cadet class in August 1942. The cadets trained at the Susanville Airport, flying planes. They lived in the Fruit Growers dormitories and took classes at the junior college next to Lassen High School. After World War I, several returning veterans began an American Legion and named it after Tommy Tucker, the first person from Susanville to die in the war. Sixteen men from Susanville died in World War I. Later a memorial building was built, which served as a meeting place and hall for festivities. Forty-nine servicemen were honored by the war department for their service during World War II. Besides involvement with the navy's cadet training program, the army built an installation between Susanville and Reno, Nevada. This installation had a prisoner of war camp consisting of Italian men. The camp was not closed off to outsiders, and many of the lumber mill workers of Italian descent remember mingling with the men in Herlong or in Susanville. (Courtesy Lassen Historical Museum.)

Olin Johnson was sheriff from 1935 to 1960. Prohibition was over, and neighbors near the county jail complained of the noise coming from the inmates housed there. One problem was the sale of liquor to Native Americans. In the 1856 meeting of local residents to set up a government, law number six stated that "no person shall sell or trade liquor to the Indians." New residents to Susanville remember that this law was still abided by in the late 1940s and 1950s. (Courtesy Lassen County Sheriff Office, Si Bollinger.)

This 1945 picture shows the A. J. Mathews family in the living room on Christmas Eve. Mathews was mayor of Susanville and a state assemblyman. He was involved in many of the business endeavors of the city, including the beginning of Lassen Lumber and Box Company and the paving of streets in Susanville. (Courtesy Lassen Historical Museum.)

Taken in 1949, this picture shows the Susanville Fire Department. All the men are volunteers including the fire chief, Fred Deal, in the middle. The men of the city truly believed in practicing their civic duty. Three fire trucks are parked behind the men. The building to the left is the fire hall located on North Lassen Street. The fire department began in the early days out of necessity and employed a bucket brigade. Then a hose cart was bought to help fight fires, and a fire hall was built soon after. (Courtesy Lassen Historical Museum.)

This picture shows Med Arnold and friends out fishing. Among those pictured are Jim McKahn, who began the first radio station, which eventually became KSUE, and Bruno Mauferdene, a jewelry store owner. Med Arnold, a grandson of Isaac Roop, was a coach and teacher at Lassen High School. Med served as city police judge and U.S. commissioner. He was very active in the founding of the Lassen Historical Society and Museum. (Courtesy Lassen Historical Museum.)

Pictured above is Ignacio Urrutia working in his new grocery store on the corner of South Spring and Main Streets. The picture below shows Ignacio working in Royal Grocery on the same corner. The first documented grocery store in the Milwood Tract was the Nataqua Grocery Store, which opened in the Pray Building. The Pray Building had a rooming house upstairs. A butcher shop was opened next door by Thomas Hill in the early 1920s. In the late 1920s, Sydney Potter ran a grocery store on the corner of South Spring and Main Streets. His wife was Ruth Potter, founder of Potter's Maternity Home. Sydney sold the business to Royal Stewart, who operated the store for many years as Royal's Grocery until he sold to Ignacio Urrutia in 1968. (Courtesy Idaho Grocery.)

Ignacio Urrutia is pictured here in his store, Idaho Grocery. Ignacio was known as Mr. Idaho to the locals. He migrated from Spain to the United States and ended up in Idaho, working as a sheepherder. Urrutia eventually came to California, first working in the logging camps before the grocery business. He bought Royal Grocery from Royal Stewart in 1968 and changed the name to Idaho Grocery. Later Urrutia added custom slaughtering to the business, which serves the area ranches. Idaho Grocery is one of the few family-owned grocery stores in Susanville; most family groceries closed upon the arrival of the chain grocery store. (Courtesy Idaho Grocery.)

This picture shows the fire department float, with Fred Deal at the helm, going past the grandstand in the 1940s. There were no buildings at the fairgrounds, and the grandstands needed to be rebuilt every year. In the 1930s, the fair advisors decided to take advantage of state funds and changed the format of the fair. A livestock show became the primary focus of the fair, and the property and equipment was deeded over to the county. The fair board now had advisors in livestock, rodeo, grounds, and entertainment. The first livestock show was in August 1936. There were no buildings available for livestock, and the show was small. The first horse show was in 1938 with Abe Jensen as the chairman. No fairs took place during 1942–1945, but they continued in 1946. At this time, several other shows were added to the livestock show, including floriculture and home economics. (Courtesy Kay Dieter.)

The picture above shows a parade float with Kay Dieter playing the part of the Southern belle. Her brothers are operating a car underneath all of the finery for the float's momentum. The float won first prize in the 1949 parade. The picture at right shows Fred Deal's Shell Station located on Main Street. The Deal children used a ladder to climb to the roof. From that perch, they could sit and have a great view of the parades going down Main Street. (Courtesy Kay Dieter.)

The picture above shows Fred Deal's first shop. The sign advertises tires, which were a great commodity until better tires were manufactured. The picture below shows Deal and Davie across from Lassen High School. To the left is the White Eagle service station in the early 1940s. Fred Deal first went to business with his dad at R. Q. Deal's Garage in Litchfield. Deal began his own business around 1930 at Weatherlow and Main Streets. In 1934, he became a partner with George B. Davie and Sons and moved to the new building across from Lassen High School. Lester Davie was Deal's longtime partner in the business. Deal was a part of the sheriff's posse, which still used horses, and was a volunteer fire chief for the City of Susanville. (Courtesy Kay Dieter.)

The picture above shows the wall on the south side of Main Street after a service station tanker truck ran through it. The wall was at the top of Main Street on the corner where Cass Hunsinger's home was for many years. Many of the larger service trucks took the corner too fast and hit the wall. In the background is the service truck on its side. (Courtesy Kay Dieter.)

Pictured here is a parade in 1955. The mud wagon was made by Henderson in Stockton. Behind the wagon is Griffin's Variety Store, which sold men's clothing. The office space upstairs was changed into apartments. To the left of Griffin's Variety Store is the Odd Fellows building. Bank of America was to the right. (Courtesy Lassen Historical Museum.)

The picture above shows Millar Hardware, located between Roop and Lassen Streets on Main Street. Elton Millar began the hardware store, and for his hard work was presented a service award from the hardware industry. The picture below shows Millar at his exhibit in the fair building showcasing General Electric products to the public. The store was remodeled in 1978, and Elton's son and daughter-in-law, Doug and Lorena, took over the business. Millar Hardware was reputed for always having what community members needed, which was made possible by the full basement for storage. The Sears store in town also had a large basement; however, it was opened for a time as a roller-skating rink. At one time, the jewelry store and show store next to Millar Hardware had an aquarium in the wall that allowed customers to see into the other stores. (Courtesy Doug and Lorena Millar.)

This picture shows the State Barber Shop after a winter snowstorm. There was so much snow on the roof that the proprietors thought the roof might collapse. What did they do? They used a ladder to prop up the roof over the sidewalk. The State Barber Shop was located in the rear of the State Café. (Courtesy of Julie McQueen.)

This picture was taken of the Texaco service station near Walker's restaurant in 1958. Gas stations used to be called service stations because a customer drove up, and the gas was pumped by an employee, who also checked the fluids and tires. Phil Brownell remembers one man who always wanted his car washed even when it was below freezing outside. (Courtesy Lassen Historical Museum.)

This picture shows Lina and Tom Barclay dressed for the 100-year celebration in Susanville. Lina is wearing her grandmother's dress, which was made in 1886 in San Francisco. The top hat belonged to congressman John Raker. Lina's grandparents, Capt. E. S. Talbot and Sophia Bacon Talbot, came to Susanville in 1874. Captain Talbot was born in Maine and spent his life before coming to Susanville on the sea. Their daughter, Susan, was born aboard the *A. H. Stephens* off the coast of Peru. After arriving in Susanville, Talbot was elected judge in 1877 and, in 1881, he was appointed deputy sheriff by Sheriff Hiram Skaddan. Talbot settled in Johnstonville as a farmer. In 1880, Talbot's daughter Susan married P. J. Goumaz, who was born in Switzerland and came to the valley from Illinois. He bought 200 acres in 1866 south of Susanville, where he had a stock business. This is where Lina spent her childhood. (Courtesy Russell Brownell.)

The picture at left shows Lina Barclay (left), Phil Brownell (center), and Tom Barclay. Lina grew up on a ranch near town but stayed with relatives when she was young to go to school. Her first husband was Russell Brownell, who was involved in many of the subdivision projects surrounding Susanville with George McDow. These subdivisions became part of the city in 1947, when through election the city was extended to Fairfield Avenue. Russell served as county assessor, and the street of Russell is named for him. Lina and Russell had one son, Phil, before Russell died in 1923. Lina remarried Tom Barclay, and the family lived in the house pictured below on Court Street. Phil worked in engineering and mechanics for a major aircraft company before returning to Susanville. This job took him to South America for awhile. (Courtesy Russell Brownell.)

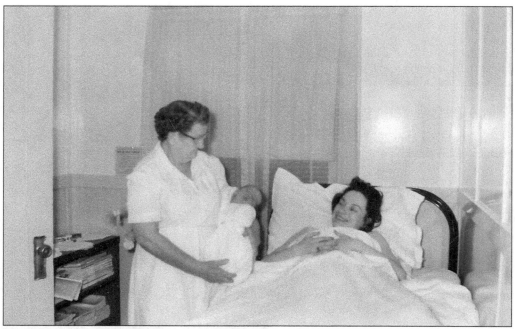

This picture shows a room inside Potter's Maternity Home. Ruth Potter is standing and holding John Weir. Marguerite Weir is in the bed. Potter's Maternity Home closed its doors in 1965. In its beginning, the home serviced women along with Riverside Hospital and the county hospital. Riverside Hospital began as the privately run hospital of the Fruit Growers Company. (Courtesy Ricki Diamond.)

Rufina Aguirre is retiring in 1975 after 20 years of service at Safeway. Aguirre began working for Safeway in 1955 after her previous employer, Lassen Lumber and Box, closed. At this time, the Safeway store operated on Roop Street. Safeway then moved to its next location, in the Main and Ash Streets' business park. (Courtesy Rufina Aguirre.)

This picture was taken in the supermarket parking lot, down the street and across from Lassen High School. To the left is the newly built high school. The old building was condemned and torn down. Susanville is still receiving lots of snow. The familiar enclosure at the corner houses a coin-operated telephone later to be removed. (Courtesy Julie McQueen.)

This class picture on the side of Lincoln School was taken about 1959. Kay Dieter is standing the second from the left. The school closed in 1967, and the Lassen National Forest Service moved in its office headquarters. Upon this school's closing, McKinley School was rebuilt on Fourth Street. Roosevelt School on Richmond Road also closed in 1967. (Courtesy Kay Dieter.)

Both pictures show the rodeo parade going down Main Street. The top picture shows the parade in 1978. Behind the car to the right is Rexall Drugs. To the left is Children's Village. Many mothers applauded the arrival of Children's Village in town because much time was spent sewing clothes for the non-average-sized child. The picture below shows Grohs store behind the horse. Besides the parades, the young people in town often enjoyed the Tennis Court Dances put on by the city. These dances were held in the 1960s to the early 1970s for the high school students. The A&W restaurant was considered the end of town. However, many of the high school students visited the Arctic Circle across Main Street from Lassen High School. Out of town near Johnstonville School was a drive-in movie theater. (Courtesy Lassen Historical Museum.)

This picture shows the sheriff's boat patrol on Eagle Lake. The *Prober* came from Lake Almanor, purchased by harbor navigation for the sheriff department. The first day on duty at Eagle Lake was June 18, 1961, and Bud West was the first person to do boat patrol. (Courtesy Lassen County Sheriff Office, Si Bollinger.)

This picture shows John Choo being awarded for membership in Safeway's elite Courtesy Club by Safeway executives in 1973. Choo came to Susanville after serving in the army during World War II. He went to work at Paul Bunyan Lumber Company before working full-time at Safeway. (Courtesy John Choo.)

This picture was taken in 1974 and shows the past presidents of the Susanville Rotary Club. Sitting from left to right are Jim Pardee, Jim McQueen, Jim Bronson, Clem Doyle, Bob Amesbury, Don Cady, and Stan Arnold. Standing from left to right are Elton Millar, Elton Davie, Ray Packwood, John Doyle, Glen Long, Bob Phillips, Ed Grant, and Jim Williams. The Susanville Rotary Club was involved in many civic projects throughout Susanville's history, including Roosevelt Pool, the annexation of the nearby subdivisions to the city, and creating Memorial Park. Bob Amesbury, a local dentist, was a prominent figure in writing some of the history of the area. Other clubs and groups have been organized. One group for the ladies is the Native Daughters of the Golden West. This group began in 1927 and promotes the preservation of local history and historic landmarks, including Peter Lassen's grave outside of town. (Courtesy Doug and Lorena Millar.)

This picture was taken on September 16, 1960, at the dedication ceremony for the California Correctional Center. Pictured from left to right are assemblywoman Pauline Davis, supervisor chairman James McQueen, governor Edmund "Pat" Brown, mayor of Susanville Elton S. Millar, state senator Stanley Arnold, and congressman "Bizz" Harold Johnson. The center was completed in 1962 and was ready to house 2,400 inmates. It was to be a minimum security prison with some inmates working for the Department of Forestry fighting fires. The center was another controversy for the townspeople. Employment was greatly needed for the area with the closing of the two large industrial lumber mills; however, the people were not sold on the idea of a prison in their backyard. Other non-local government agencies offering employment were the Lassen National Forest, the Bureau of Land Management, and state offices. (Courtesy Doug and Loren Millar.)

Visit us at
arcadiapublishing.com

·······························

Printed in the USA
CPSIA information can be obtained
at www.ICGtesting.com
LVHW071025211223
766685LV00056B/922

9 781531 637606